CONTENTS

SETTING THE SCENE

In 100 BC, at Caesar's birth, Rome was the greatest city in the ancient world, and its empire the largest since Alexander the Great.

BRITANNIA

Deal

River Thames

River Rhi

Eburone

Nervii

Agedincum

GAUL

Alesia

Avaricum

Bibracte

Gergovia

Lugdonum

Narbo

Massilia

ILERDA

SPAIN

ROME

Carthago Nova

Munda

Cadiz

MEDITERRANEAN SEA

SICILY

AFRICA

MAURETANIA

HADROMETUM

THAPSUS

✗ SITE OF MAJOR BATTLES

CONQUESTS OF CAESAR

APPROXIMATE EXTENT OF EMPIRE AT CAESAR'S DEATH, 44 BC

SCALE 1; 27 000 000

0   1000KM

0   750 MILES

the story

JULIUS CAESAR

Marcus Junius Brutus: *One of Caesar's naval commanders in Gaul. Governor of Transalpine Gaul between 48-46 BC. A ringleader of Caesar's assassination in 44 BC.*

Cleopatra: *Daughter of the Egyptian king Ptolemy XII who became Caesar's lover and bore him a son called Caesarion. Caesar made her queen of Egypt, but her later romance with the Roman general Mark Antony caused arguments with Octavian.*

Mark Antony: *One of Caesar's generals who became quaestor, tribune, then Consul in 44 BC. He joined the Second Triumvirate with Octavian and Lepidus after Caesar's death, then fought with Cleopatra against Octavian in 31 BC.*

Gaius Julius Caesar Octavianus (Augustus): *Born 63 BC, Octavian was the great nephew of Julius Caesar and became his heir and adopted son just before Caesar's death in 44 BC. Octavian joined forces with Mark Antony to defeat Caesar's murderers Cassius and Brutus at Philippi. Octavian returned to Rome and added the title Augustus to his name, becoming Rome's first emperor. He died in AD 14.*

Gaius Julius Caesar: *He Became the first Emperor of Rome. He was born on 13 July, 100 BC at a time when the Roman Empire was expanding at a great pace. He was born into a noble family, and forged a distinguished career as a general and leader. Caesar was responsible for conquering Gaul and defeating various uprisings at home. His life was brought to an end at the hands of jealous Roman senators in 44 BC."*

Vercingetorix: *Member of the Gallic Arverni tribe. A brave and canny warrior, he formed and led a confederation of the Gauls in a rebellion against Rome. He was defeated by and surrendered to Caesar at Alesia in 52 BC, and was paraded in Caesar's Gallic triumph in Rome.*

Copyright © ticktock Entertainment Ltd. 2006
First published in Great Britain in 2006 by ticktock Media Ltd.,
Unit 2, Orchard Business Centre, North Farm Road, Tunbridge Wells, Kent, TN2 3XF
ISBN 1 84696 005 3
Printed in China
A CIP catalogue record for this book is available from the British Library.

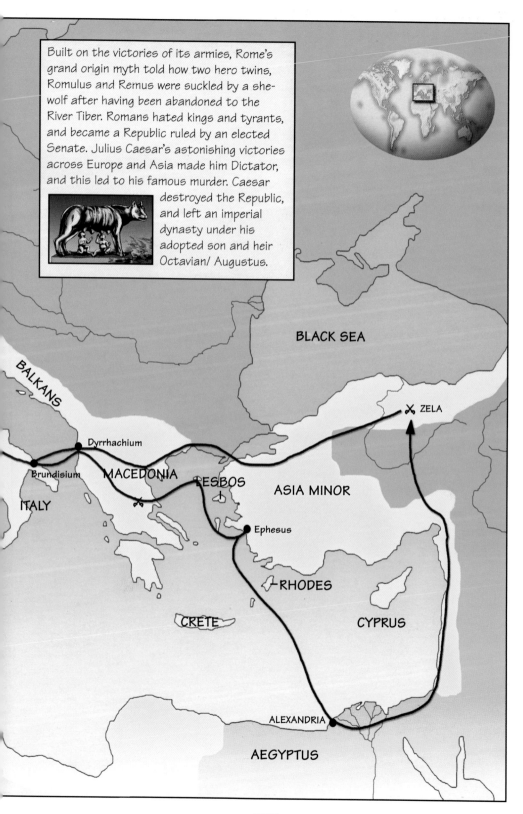

Built on the victories of its armies, Rome's grand origin myth told how two hero twins, Romulus and Remus were suckled by a she-wolf after having been abandoned to the River Tiber. Romans hated kings and tyrants, and became a Republic ruled by an elected Senate. Julius Caesar's astonishing victories across Europe and Asia made him Dictator, and this led to his famous murder. Caesar destroyed the Republic, and left an imperial dynasty under his adopted son and heir Octavian/ Augustus.

BLACK SEA

BALKANS

Dyrrhachium

Brundisium

MACEDONIA

ITALY

LESBOS

ASIA MINOR

ZELA

Ephesus

RHODES

CRETE

CYPRUS

ALEXANDRIA

AEGYPTUS

BIRTH OF A KING

Caesar's birth to an impoverished patrician family was an unremarkable event. Nevertheless, his family's status enabled him to gain important offices of state at an early age. His father's death, his marriage to Cornelia, and the Dictatorship of Sulla in Rome were formative events in Caesar's early years.

Gaius Julius Caesar was born on 12 or 13 July in either 102 or 100 BC in the multi-ethnic neighbourhood of Rome known as Subura. His mother Aurelia, presented their son to his father, the Roman magistrate Gaius Caesar.

'Gaius, husband, look at your handsome son – we have been blessed by the gods'.

'Gaius, my son and heir. You have your mother's beauty and your family's good fortune!

Caesar's mother took great care over her son's upbringing. She paid for him to be educated by one of Rome's best teachers – Marcus Antonius Gnipho – who also taught the famous orator Cicero.

FAST FACT Caesar was Julius's family name, though after his death it was adopted by later emperors as a title. Its ancient prestige saw it adopted as a royal title in Russia (Czar), and in Germany (Kaiser).

In 88 BC, when Julius Caesar was 12 years old, the Roman general Sulla marched on Rome. He captured the city, and strengthened the Roman Senate.

'**Run, run!** Sulla the Dictator has seized Rome!'

'**Look!** See how Rome's invincible legions flee before us!'

The social unrest in Rome gave the Asian king Mithridates the opportunity to wage war in Asia Minor (modern Turkey). Mithridates massacred many Romans during the uprising and caused panic in Rome.

'**Quick!** We must escape. King Mithridates will kill us all!'

In 87 BC, aged 13, the young Julius Caesar was given the lifetime honour of being appointed the High Priest of Jupiter in Rome.

Overlooked by the great statue of Jupiter in the god's own temple, Julius Caesar was given the robes of his new office.

'Gaius Julius Caesar – you are now the chosen one – the High Priest of Jupiter'

'I will honour Jupiter and Rome. My family will be proud of me'

FAST FACT Roman religion, a mix of old Etruscan beliefs and re-named Greek gods, was political and spiritual. Caesar's appointment as flamen dialis (High Priest) of Jupiter (equivalent to Greek Zeus) showed how religious offices were used to further an individual's political career.

In 85 BC, when he was 15 years old, Julius Caesar became a man according to Roman law. In a traditional ceremony, his father gave him the toga virilis to wear as a sign of manhood.

'Gaius – you are a man now. Take the toga and wear it proudly!'

'Father, I am honoured. I am now truly a Roman'

Roman men dominated society, and Roman law kept women at a disadvantage. Even at a young age, patrician boys such as Caesar were already being groomed for a political future by being awarded important offices of state.

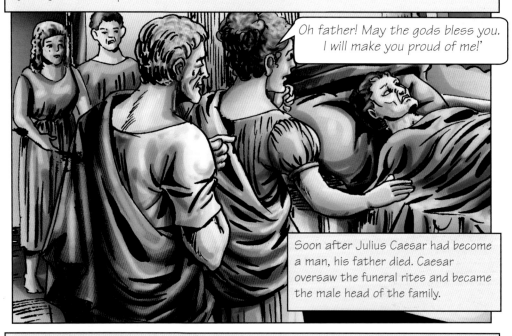

Soon after Julius Caesar had become a man, his father died. Caesar oversaw the funeral rites and became the male head of the family.

Aged 16, Julius Caesar married for the first time. Cornelia, his wife, was the daughter of the general Lucius Cornelius Cinna who ruled Rome until Sulla recaptured it in 82 BC.

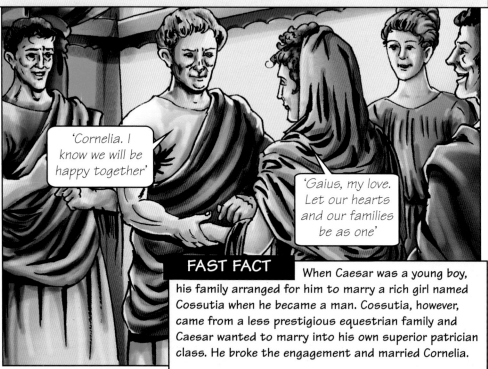

FAST FACT When Caesar was a young boy, his family arranged for him to marry a rich girl named Cossutia when he became a man. Cossutia, however, came from a less prestigious equestrian family and Caesar wanted to marry into his own superior patrician class. He broke the engagement and married Cornelia.

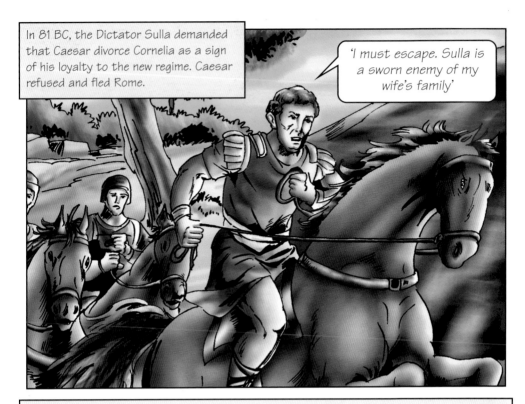

In 81 BC, the Dictator Sulla demanded that Caesar divorce Cornelia as a sign of his loyalty to the new regime. Caesar refused and fled Rome.

'I must escape. Sulla is a sworn enemy of my wife's family'

Later the same year, Sulla was persuaded to forgive Caesar who returned to Rome, but was stripped of his office of High Priest of Jupiter. Sulla also seized Caesar's wealth, including his inheritance and Cornelia's dowry.

'By order of Sulla, Dictator of Rome, Gaius Julius Caesar is no longer High Priest of Jupiter'

Also in 81 BC, Julius Caesar and Cornelia had a baby daughter, named Julia, who would be Caesar's only legal child.

'What a beautiful daughter. The goddess Venus has smiled on us both'

'Husband, may our child Julia do honour to both our families'

Caesar's lack of male child would change the Roman Empire when he had to adopt Octavian his great nephew as his heir later in life.

FAST FACT Sulla's anger at Caesar was a dangerous low point in Caesar's life. Every night, Caesar slept in a different house, bribing the owner to hide him from Sulla's secret police.

A MILITARY CAREER

In 80 BC, the 20-year old Caesar began his military career. He left Rome and travelled to Asia Minor where he served for several years under the praetor (provincial governor) Marcus Thermus.

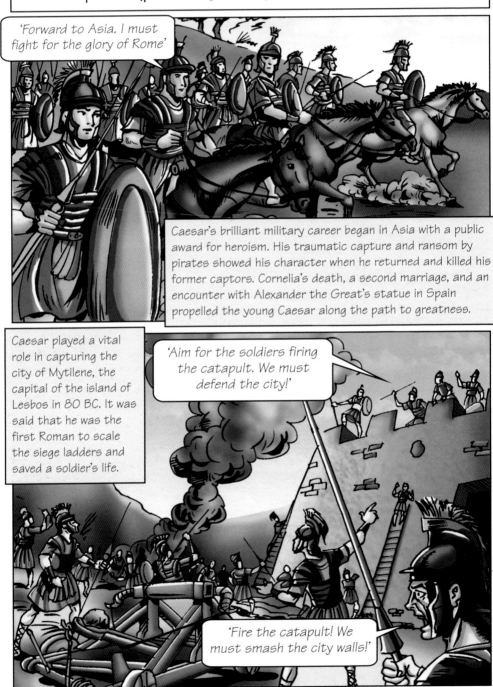

'Forward to Asia. I must fight for the glory of Rome'

Caesar's brilliant military career began in Asia with a public award for heroism. His traumatic capture and ransom by pirates showed his character when he returned and killed his former captors. Cornelia's death, a second marriage, and an encounter with Alexander the Great's statue in Spain propelled the young Caesar along the path to greatness.

Caesar played a vital role in capturing the city of Mytilene, the capital of the island of Lesbos in 80 BC. It was said that he was the first Roman to scale the siege ladders and saved a soldier's life.

'Aim for the soldiers firing the catapult. We must defend the city!'

'Fire the catapult! We must smash the city walls!'

At Mytilene, Caesar's bravery won him the right to wear a crown of oak leaves and acorns for his heroism during the fighting. He wore it for the rest of his life, to show his reputation but also to hide his thinning hair which soon turned to baldness.

When Rome heard of Caesar's victory, he was awarded a permanent seat in the Senate without any age restrictions.

FAST FACT During Caesar's military service in Asia, he is said to have had a homosexual affair with Nicomedes IV, king of Bithynia. Caesar's enemies never let him forget this one scandal and stain on his character.

15

In 75 BC, at the age of 25, Caesar sailed to Rhodes to study rhetoric. He was captured en route by the pirates who infested the eastern Mediterranean.

The pirates demanded the usual ransom of 6,000 gold pieces, but Caesar insisted that as he was an aristocrat this should be doubled. It took forty days for his followers to raise the money and gain his freedom.

Caesar had warned the pirates that once free he would return, and capture and crucify them all. Within a few months he had kept his promise.

'Casear kept his promise. We will all be killed now'

After having defeated the pirates, Caesar sailed on to Rhodes where he began his lessons in rhetoric under the famous scholar Apollonius Molon.

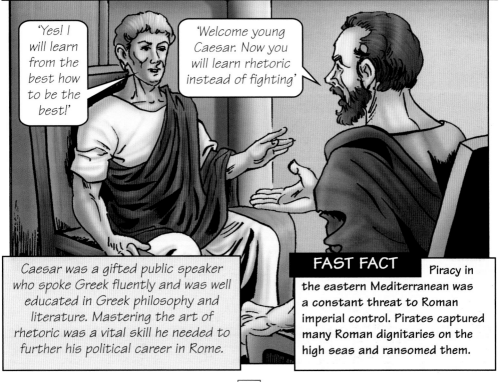

'Yes! I will learn from the best how to be the best!'

'Welcome young Caesar. Now you will learn rhetoric instead of fighting'

Caesar was a gifted public speaker who spoke Greek fluently and was well educated in Greek philosophy and literature. Mastering the art of rhetoric was a vital skill he needed to further his political career in Rome.

FAST FACT Piracy in the eastern Mediterranean was a constant threat to Roman imperial control. Pirates captured many Roman dignitaries on the high seas and ransomed them.

At the age of 31, Caesar is appointed quaestor (finance officer) and campaigned against the tribes of Spain in 69 BC.

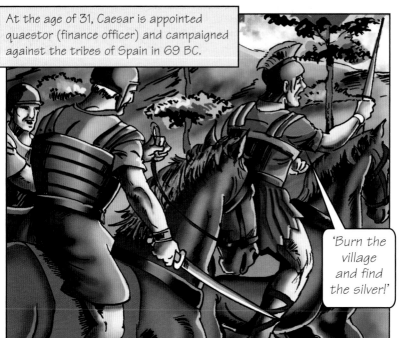

'Burn the village and find the silver!'

When in Gades (modern Cadiz), Caesar saw a statue to Alexander the Great in the Temple of Heracles. Caesar is said to have wept because while Alexander had conquered a great empire at the same age, Caesar himself had accomplished little.

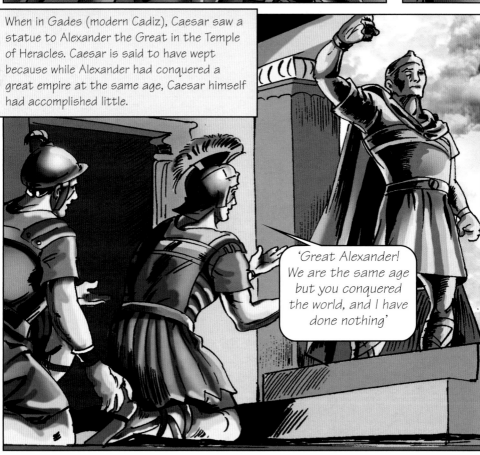

'Great Alexander! We are the same age but you conquered the world, and I have done nothing'

'I praise the family of my Aunt Julia. She was noble and just, a true mother of Rome'

Caesar resigned his quaestorship and returned to Rome. He gave a grand speech at the funeral of his aunt Julia, and praised her family's descent from the gods of Rome. In so doing he also praised himself, as her family was his.

Soon after Julia's funeral, Caesar's own wife Cornelia died. He organized the traditional funeral ceremony, and once again grieved at the loss of a loved one.

'Cornelia, my beloved wife. I promise to look after our daughter Julia'

FAST FACT Alexander the Great's extraordinary victories and conquests inspired the great generals of Rome who saw themselves as his successors as masters of the ancient world. Pompey, Caesar, and later emperors such as Caligula measured their lives by Alexander's achievements.

19

Caesar married for a second time at the age of 33 in 67 BC. His new wife was Pompeia, the granddaughter of the Dictator Sulla and a relative of Rome's famous general Pompey the Great.

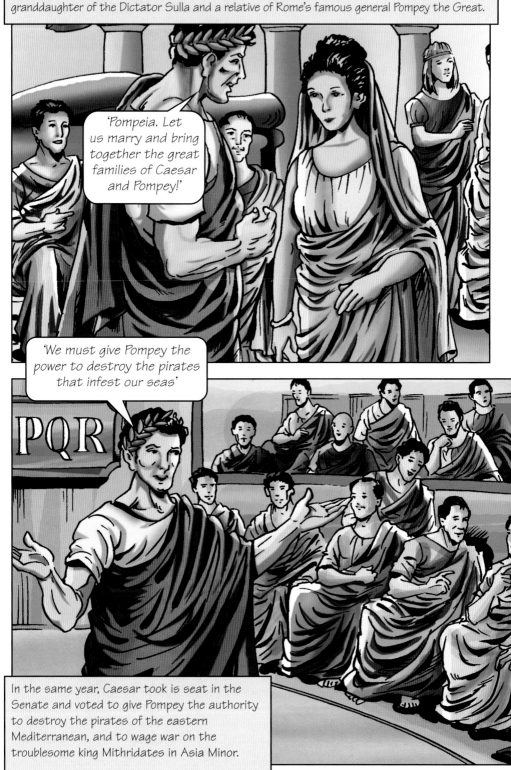

'Pompeia. Let us marry and bring together the great families of Caesar and Pompey!'

'We must give Pompey the power to destroy the pirates that infest our seas'

In the same year, Caesar took is seat in the Senate and voted to give Pompey the authority to destroy the pirates of the eastern Mediterranean, and to wage war on the troublesome king Mithridates in Asia Minor.

In 65 BC, Caesar became a magistrate (curule aedile) in Rome, and controlled the city's markets, temples, and public buildings.

'We must beautify Rome with new buildings'

Caesar's duties also included supervising and sponsoring Rome's public holidays and games. He organized a huge event in which 320 pairs of gladiators, dressed in silver armour, fought each other and wild animals.

Aaargh

'Quick! Stab the lion in the heart!'

FAST FACT Caesar knew well how to appeal to Rome's population by organizing chariot races and gladiatorial contests. Such spectacular events were the mass entertainment of the day, and Caesar's reputation soared when he spent vast amounts on paying for them.

POLITICAL PACTS

Caesar's re-election to High Priest of Jupiter was a crucial political achievement. Caesar now had a vast wealth, looted from Spain. He became Consul in 40 BC, and forged a political pact with Pompey and Crassus, the empire's wealthiest man. Together they ruled the empire.

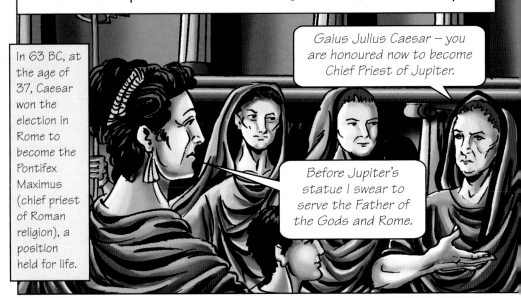

In 63 BC, at the age of 37, Caesar won the election in Rome to become the Pontifex Maximus (chief priest of Roman religion), a position held for life.

Gaius Julius Caesar – you are honoured now to become Chief Priest of Jupiter.

Before Jupiter's statue I swear to serve the Father of the Gods and Rome.

Caesar divorced his wife Pompeia for not being above suspicion. in accusations that she was unfaithful to him with one of her husband's young friends, Publius Pulcher.

'Go! Guilty or not - Caesar's wife must be above suspicion!'

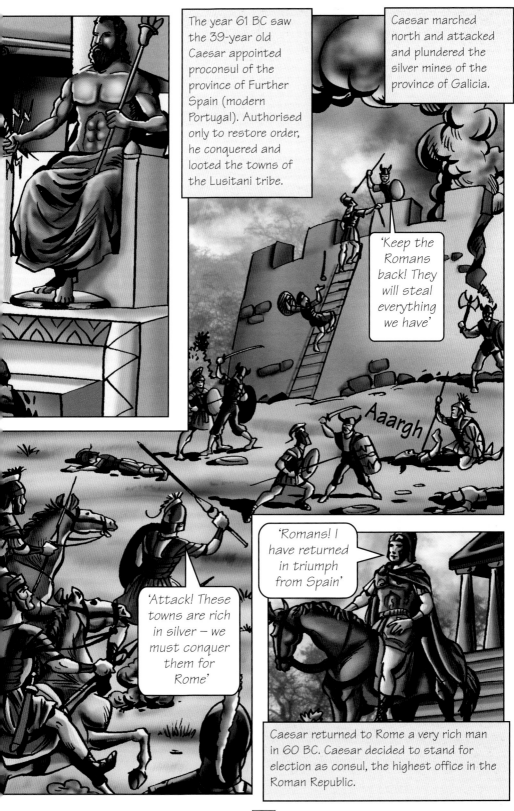

The year 61 BC saw the 39-year old Caesar appointed proconsul of the province of Further Spain (modern Portugal). Authorised only to restore order, he conquered and looted the towns of the Lusitani tribe.

Caesar marched north and attacked and plundered the silver mines of the province of Galicia.

'Keep the Romans back! They will steal everything we have'

Aaargh

'Attack! These towns are rich in silver — we must conquer them for Rome'

'Romans! I have returned in triumph from Spain'

Caesar returned to Rome a very rich man in 60 BC. Caesar decided to stand for election as consul, the highest office in the Roman Republic.

At the age of 40, in December 60 BC, Caesar won the Consulship of Rome with the help of Pompey and Marcus Licinius Crassus, Rome's richest man.

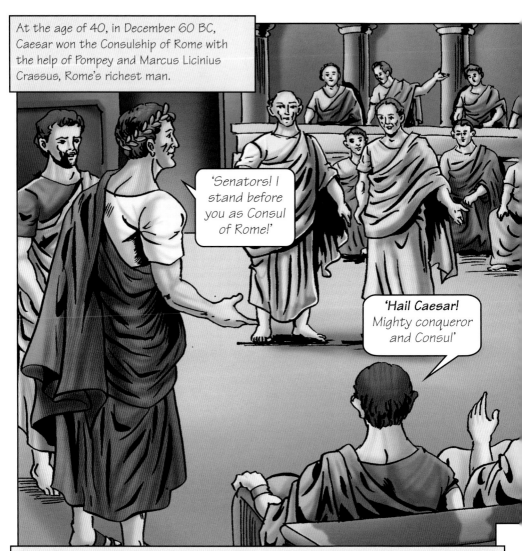

'Senators! I stand before you as Consul of Rome!'

'Hail Caesar! Mighty conqueror and Consul'

Caesar also repaid Pompey's support and won the gratitude of the Army and Rome's poor when he gave land to Pompey's veteran soldiers and the city's lower classes.

'Take this land as a reward for your services to Rome!'

When Caesar's sworn enemy, the famous Roman orator Cato the Younger, opposed Caesar in the Senate he was dragged from his seat on Caesar's orders and thrown into jail.

Caesar, together with Pompey and Crassus, became the three great masters of Rome in 60 BC. Their period of political control became known as the First Triumvirate.

'My friends Pompey and Crassus! We three now rule Rome'

In 59 BC, Caesar married for the third time. His new wife was Calpurnia, the daughter of Lucius Calpunius Piso, a close friend of Crassus.

Calpurnia – our marriage will bind us and safeguard the future of Rome

'Yes Caesar! We shall be happy and so shall everyone in Rome'

Caesar's marriage was a political alliance above all. It sealed Caesar's relationship with Crassus, and rewarded Piso who took over as Consul in 58 BC.

In the same year that Caesar married Calpurnia, Pompey married Caesar's daughter Julia. The First Triumvirate was a group of men connected by marriage as well as personal ambition and power.

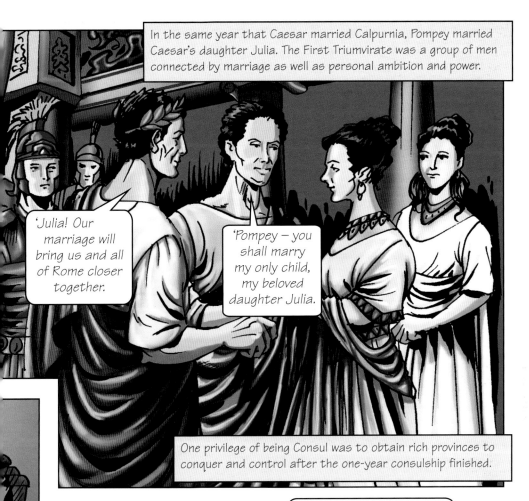

'Julia! Our marriage will bring us and all of Rome closer together.

'Pompey – you shall marry my only child, my beloved daughter Julia.

One privilege of being Consul was to obtain rich provinces to conquer and control after the one-year consulship finished.

Legions of Rome! We will conquer all of Gaul for the empire.

In 59 BC, Caesar arranged that he be given Illyricum (Dalmatian Coast), Cisalpine Gaul (northern Italy), and Transalpine Gaul (southern France). A year later he left Rome and rode north to take command of Gaul.

FAMOUS WARS

Caesar's most famous wars were against the Gauls between 58 and 52 BC, and his defeat of the Gallic chieftain Vercingetorix his most important victory. He invaded Britain and Germany twice, and crossed the Rubicon river to become master of Rome as Pompey fled to the Balkans. Caesar was hailed as Dictator.

We must stop the Helvetii before they invade Gaul and cause havoc.

Follow your standard for the Senate and People of Rome!

Caesar's famous Gallic Wars began in 58 BC when he marched north and attacked the Helvetii (a Swiss tribe) and stopped their invasion of central Gaul. He then defeated the Germanic leader Ariovistus who had recently invaded Gaul.

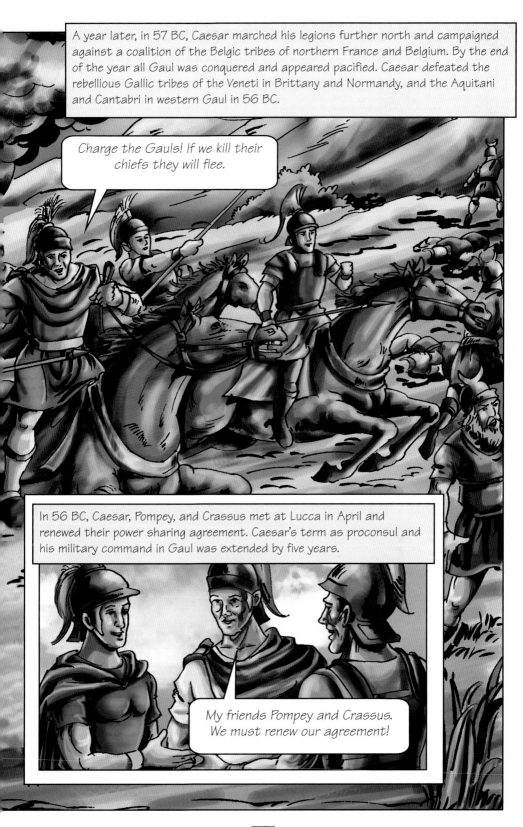

A year later, in 57 BC, Caesar marched his legions further north and campaigned against a coalition of the Belgic tribes of northern France and Belgium. By the end of the year all Gaul was conquered and appeared pacified. Caesar defeated the rebellious Gallic tribes of the Veneti in Brittany and Normandy, and the Aquitani and Cantabri in western Gaul in 56 BC.

Charge the Gauls! If we kill their chiefs they will flee.

In 56 BC, Caesar, Pompey, and Crassus met at Lucca in April and renewed their power sharing agreement. Caesar's term as proconsul and his military command in Gaul was extended by five years.

My friends Pompey and Crassus. We must renew our agreement!

In 55 BC, Caesar became the first Roman to cross the River Rhine and invade Germany. He was angered by the Germanic tribes' support for the Belgic tribes in Gaul. Caesar spent 18 days ravaging German territory and intimidating the local population.

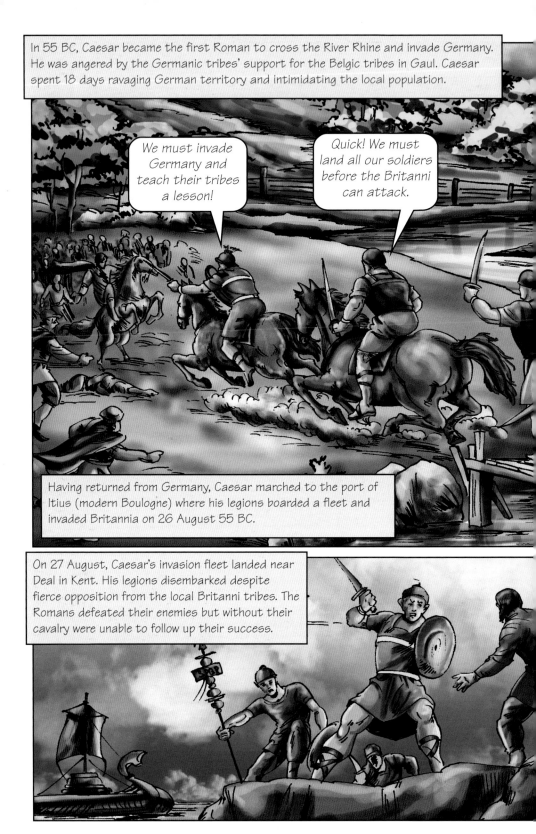

We must invade Germany and teach their tribes a lesson!

Quick! We must land all our soldiers before the Britanni can attack.

Having returned from Germany, Caesar marched to the port of Itius (modern Boulogne) where his legions boarded a fleet and invaded Britannia on 26 August 55 BC.

On 27 August, Caesar's invasion fleet landed near Deal in Kent. His legions disembarked despite fierce opposition from the local Britanni tribes. The Romans defeated their enemies but without their cavalry were unable to follow up their success.

Caesar campaigned against the Britanni tribes for several weeks. The tribes surrendered and rebelled several times. After their final submission, Caesar returned to Gaul with his legions.

Burn their farms and destroy the village!

What devilry is this? They are using chariots in battle!

The Romans have few horses — we must ride them down!

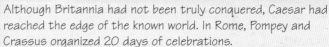

Although Britannia had not been truly conquered, Caesar had reached the edge of the known world. In Rome, Pompey and Crassus organized 20 days of celebrations.

Hail Caesar! Rome shall celebrate his victories for 20 days!

Between 55 and 52 BC, riots and political unrest occurred in Rome, and Caesar campaigned in Gaul. He returned to Britannia in 54 BC, and crossed the River Thames near London. He also crossed the Rhine for a second time a year later.

In 52 BC, a confederation of Gallic tribes under the formidable leader Vercingetorix rebelled against Roman rule. Roman towns in Gaul were burned down and their inhabitants massacred.

We Gauls shall never surrender to Rome!

Caesar finally trapped Vercingetorix in the hill-fort town of Alesia in central Gaul, and defeated attempts by other Celtic tribes to join the rebel leader. Caesar surrounded the fort with huge defensive ditches and towers and finally defeated Vercingetorix's forces.

Vercingetorix surrendered, and the day after the battle he dressed himself in his finest armour and rode into Caesar's camp. The Gallic leader threw away his arms and armour and sat motionless at Caesar's feet. The rebellion was over.

'Great Caesar you have won. I surrender on behalf of all the tribes.

You fought bravely Vercingetorix. Now Gaul belongs to Rome.

By 51 BC, Caesar was victorious in Gaul but in trouble in Rome where many feared he wanted to make himself King. On 10 January 49 BC, Caesar marched with his army into Italy in what was an act of war.

'We must cross the Rubicon into Italy and save Rome from Pompey'

The Senate had mistakenly thought that Italian cities would reject Caesar, but they surrendered to him as he passed.

'Welcome Caesar - hero of Gaul!'

'Hurry! We must reach Rome before Pompey escapes'

Pompey fled Rome with his soldiers and senators. He marched south to Brundisium (Brinidisi), intending to sail for the Balkans and raise new armies in the East. In the rush to escape Rome, Pompey forgot to take the imperial treasury.

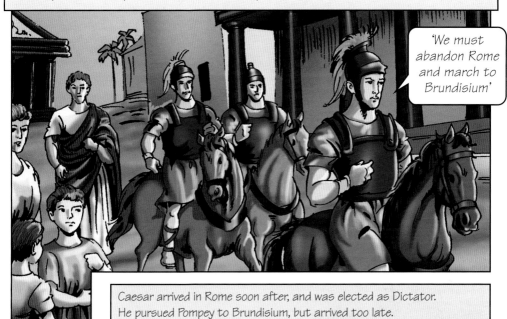

'We must abandon Rome and march to Brundisium'

Caesar arrived in Rome soon after, and was elected as Dictator. He pursued Pompey to Brundisium, but arrived too late.

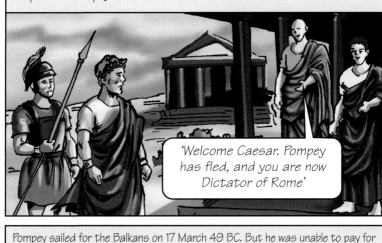

'Welcome Caesar. Pompey has fled, and you are now Dictator of Rome'

Pompey sailed for the Balkans on 17 March 49 BC. But he was unable to pay for armies to bribe the Eastern kings he had established in power.

'Sail to the east where we shall raise a new army against Caesar'

TOWARDS THE END

Caesar's defeat of Pompey in 49 BC left him the most powerful man in the empire. His affair with Cleopatra made her Queen of Egypt and gave Caesar a son – Caesarion. Caesar's election as Dictator for Life led to his assassination in 44 BC and the empire passed to his adopted son and heir Octavian – the future emperor Augustus. On the 4 January 48 BC, Caesar sailed for the Balkans with only half his legions due to his lack of transport ships.

On 9 August 49 BC, Pompey and Caesar clashed again at the town of Pharsalus. Although Pompey had more troops, he was outwitted and outmanoeuvred by Caesar. Caesar marched his legions south into central Greece to find food and rest his troops. Pompey was prematurely hailed as Imperator (Emperor), and chased Caesar to fight a decisive battle.

'Caesar is upon us! We must retreat. Warn Pompey!'

'Fight loyal Romans! We will defeat Pompey this day'

'Caesar look! Pompey's men are fleeing'

Pompey fled the Pharsalus battlefield and sailed to Egypt where he expected a friendly welcome from his young client king Ptolemy XIII. Instead he was stabbed and decapitated.

'Great Pompey – you must die now.'

'Romans! You betray me'

Caesar arrived in Alexandria on 2 October and was presented with Pompey's severed head and his signet ring. Caesar was angered not pleased by Ptolemy XIII's actions.

'Welcome Caesar. Here is a gift – the head of your enemy!'

'Welcome Cleopatra! We must talk of your future'

Cleopatra, Ptolemy XIII's sister and rival for the Egyptian throne, seduced Caesar by famously being presented to him rolled up in a linen sack. They started a long and infamous love affair.

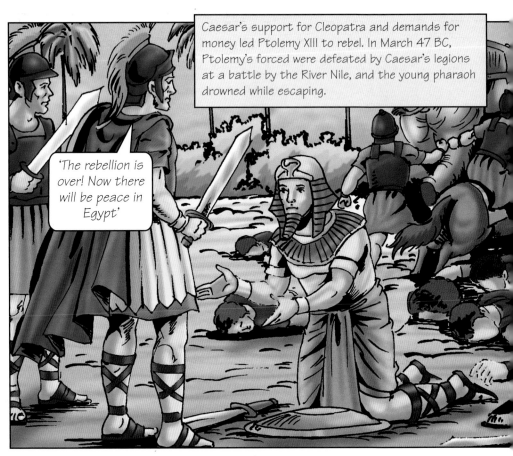

Caesar's support for Cleopatra and demands for money led Ptolemy XIII to rebel. In March 47 BC, Ptolemy's forced were defeated by Caesar's legions at a battle by the River Nile, and the young pharaoh drowned while escaping.

'The rebellion is over! Now there will be peace in Egypt'

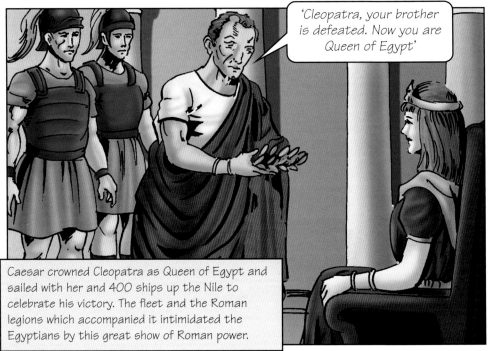

'Cleopatra, your brother is defeated. Now you are Queen of Egypt'

Caesar crowned Cleopatra as Queen of Egypt and sailed with her and 400 ships up the Nile to celebrate his victory. The fleet and the Roman legions which accompanied it intimidated the Egyptians by this great show of Roman power.

In June 47 BC, aged 53, Caesar marched north and defeated the rebellious King Pharnaces II of Pontus (northern Turkey) (Mithridates' son) at the Battle of Zela.

'I came, I saw, I conquered! Asia once more belongs to Rome'

With Pharnaces defeated and Asia Minor pacified, Caesar sailed for Rome.

'Caesarion, my child. One day you will be ruler of Rome and Egypt!'

On 23 June 47 BC, Cleopatra gave birth to Caesar's son in Alexandria where she had been left under the protection of three Roman legions. The baby boy was called Caesarion.

When Caesar arrived back in Rome the Senate appointed him Dictator for his victory against Pharnaces. He created many new senators from his army and supporters, and held several magnificent triumphs.

'Welcome Caesar! We appoint you Dictator for Life for your services to Rome'

'Great Senate of Rome – I bring victories from Greece, Egypt and Asia'

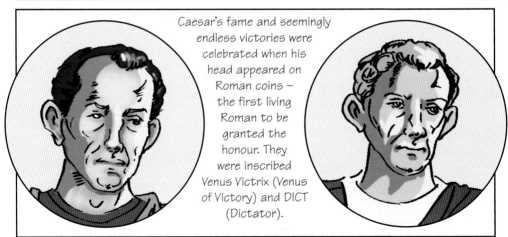

Caesar's fame and seemingly endless victories were celebrated when his head appeared on Roman coins – the first living Roman to be granted the honour. They were inscribed Venus Victrix (Venus of Victory) and DICT (Dictator).

'Astronomers listen! We shall reorganize the calendar and I shall have a new month named after myself – July!'

Caesar was interested in administration as well as war. With the help of Cleopatra's astrologer, he reorganized the old Roman calendar to have 365 days with a leap year every 4 years. This new Julian calendar stayed in use until 1582.

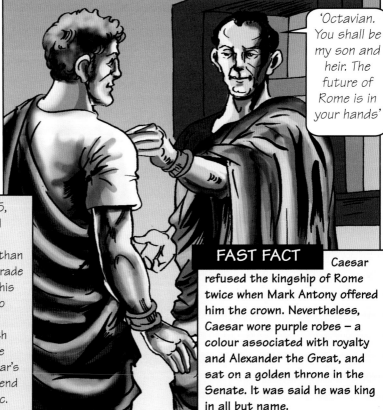

'Octavian. You shall be my son and heir. The future of Rome is in your hands'

In 45 BC, aged 55, Caesar appointed his great nephew Octavian, rather than his patrician comrade Mark Antony, as his heir. Octavian also became Caesar's adopted son. Both moves marked the beginning of Caesar's dynasty and the end of the old Republic.

FAST FACT

Caesar refused the kingship of Rome twice when Mark Antony offered him the crown. Nevertheless, Caesar wore purple robes – a colour associated with royalty and Alexander the Great, and sat on a golden throne in the Senate. It was said he was king in all but name.

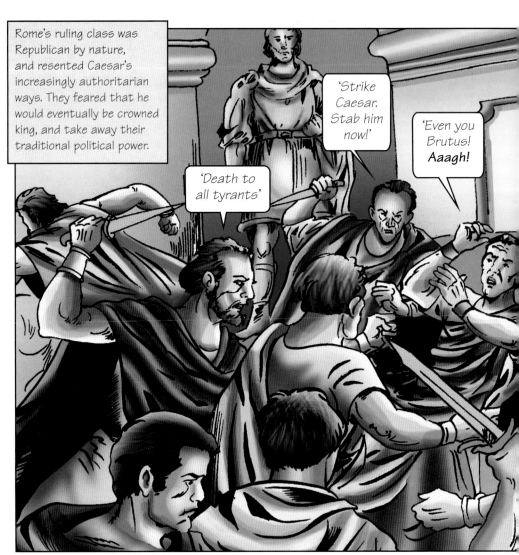

Rome's ruling class was Republican by nature, and resented Caesar's increasingly authoritarian ways. They feared that he would eventually be crowned king, and take away their traditional political power.

'Strike Caesar. Stab him now!'

'Even you Brutus! **Aaagh!**'

'Death to all tyrants'

Several days later, Caesar's funeral took place in Rome's Forum and Mark Antony gave the funeral oration before throwing a torch onto the pyre. The crowd threw clothing and furniture onto the fire in their grief for the greatest Roman.

'Caesar is dead! Our hero, our god. Murdered not by Gauls but by Romans!'

Caesar had to be killed if he was to be stopped. A noted Republican, Marcus Brutus was persuaded to join Cassius Longinus and 60 other conspirators in the murder.

After Caesar's death, Mark Antony and Octavian joined forces and defeated Cassius and Brutus in battle at Philippi in Macedonia. It was said that Cassius committed suicide with the same dagger he used to murder Caesar.

'Legions of Rome – attack and slay the murderers of Caesar'

Caesar may have suspected a conspiracy. But on the Ides of March (15 March) 44 BC, he attended a Senate meeting in Pompey's Theatre and was stabbed to death by the assassins.

'I am Caesar's son, ruler of Rome, and Augustus'

Octavian argued with, then defeated the forces of Mark Antony and his new lover Queen Cleopatra, both of whom committed suicide in Alexandria. Octavian returned to Rome, added the title Augustus to his name and ruled as emperor until he died in AD 14.

Julius Caesar's life was long and violent. It was packed with endless battles across the ancient world and murderous political intrigues in Rome. Caesar's skill was as a brilliant general but also a ruthless politician. It is impossible to include every aspect of such a life in one book. This timeline and fast fact section fills in some of the gaps in Caesar's remarkable life that changed forever the shape of the Mediterranean world.

July 13, 102 or 100 BC (sources differ): *Birth of Gaius Julius Caesar*

87: *Julius Caesar, aged 13, chosen as High Priest of Jupiter*

84: *Caesar's first marriage to Cornelia, daughter of Cinna.*

81: *Caesar flees Rome to escape the hostility of Roman Dictator Sulla. Caesar and Cornelia have a daughter, Julia.*

80: *Caesar leaves Rome for military service in Asia Minor and wins the oak-leaf crown for his bravery at the siege of Mytilene on Lesbos. Caesar permitted to sit in the Roman Senate.*

74: *Caesar fights against Mithridates's forces in Asia and returns to Rome.*

69: *Caesar's wife Cornelia dies.*

67: *Caesar's second marriage to Pompeia, Sulla's granddaughter.*

63: *Caesar wins election in Rome to become Pontifex Maximus.*

62: *Caesar wins the office of praetor in Rome and divorces his wife Pompeia after a scandal.*

60: *Caesar forms the First Triumvirate with Pompey and Crassus.*

59: *Caesar marries his third wife, Calpurnia, the daughter of Piso.*

58: *Caesar begins his Gallic Wars.*

57: *Caesar and his legions fight the Belgic tribes of northern Gaul.*

56: *The triumvirate is renewed at Lucca*

55: *Caesar's proconsulship in Gaul extended for 5 years. He crosses the Rhine and then briefly invades Britain.*

54: *Caesar continues fighting in Gaul and campaigns a second time in Britain.*

53: *Caesar campaigns against rebellious Gallic tribes.*

52: *Caesar victorious against Gauls. The Gallic rebellion crumbles.*

48: *Caesar routs Pompey at the Battle of Pharsalus on 9 August. Caesar arrives in Alexandria and meets Cleopatra.*

47: *Caesar elected Dictator again, defeats Egyptian army under Ptolemy XIII, and destroys the rebellion of Pharnaces II at Zela in Asia Minor. Cleopatra gives birth to Caesar's son, Caesarion.*

46: *Caesar elected Consul for third time. He defeats Pompeian forces at the Battle of Thapsus, and is elected Dictator for 10 years.*

45: *Roman Senate elect Caesar Dictator for life and his image appears on coins. Octavian becomes his heir and adopted son.*

44: *Caesar refuses to be crowned king. He is murdered by Cassius, Brutus and 60 other conspirators on the Ides of March (15 March) in a Senate meeting.*

42: *Caesar is deified, and Cassius and Brutus commit suicide after being defeated by Octavian and Mark Antony at Philippi.*

DID YOU KNOW?

1 *The Roman Empire in Caesar's lifetime extended from Gaul (France) in the north, south to Spain, and east to Asia (Turkey), Egypt, and Palestine. It was the largest empire since Alexander the Great (356-323 BC).*

 2 *The Roman army excelled in military discipline, tactics, and the machinery of war. Roman siege engines and towers destroyed enemy fortresses, and the testudo (tortoise) formation allowed legionaries to link their shields together and advance in safety.*

3 *The Roman Empire was built on slavery. 150,000 captives were sold as slaves after just one battle in Macedonia in 168 BC. Slaves could be killed or freed by their masters. By AD 400, 8 of 10 Roman families had slave ancestry in their lineage.*

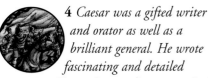 **4** *Caesar was a gifted writer and orator as well as a brilliant general. He wrote fascinating and detailed memoirs of his military campaigns, which were also excellent propaganda for his political aspirations. Most famous is his account of the Gallic Wars.*

5 *Caesar's victories in Gaul were his greatest military achievement. He stormed 800 cities, vanquished 300 tribes, killed one million Gauls, took another million prisoner, and sold a further million into slavery.*

 6 *Campaigning in Britannia (Britain), Caesar observed that few inhabitants sowed corn, most lived on milk and meat, and that they wore animal skins and painted themselves blue to enhance their fierce appearance.*

7 *The predictable annual flooding of the Nile made Egypt a very rich agricultural land. Fleets of grain ships sailed from Alexandria to Rome.*

8 *During his 9 months in Alexandria, Caesar was not impressed by the city's magnificence other than the tomb of Alexander the Great.*

9 *To make himself popular at Rome, Caesar began many new buildings in 46 BC. These included a new Senate House, a great marketplace called the Basilica Julia, a new state library, and a temple to his ancestor, the goddess Venus.*

10 *At the Battle of Thapsus (46 BC),* *near Carthage in North Africa, Caesar destroyed the last remaining Republican forces of Pompey. The Republican orator Cato committed suicide after this.*

11 *Caesar was elected Dictator four times, the last was in 44 BC just before his death, when he became Dictator for Life. He was assassinated during a meeting of the Senate. At the time, the building itself was being rebuilt with Caesar's own money. In 42 BC, Caesar was defied.*

12 *Augustus used his imperial power to enact many of Caesar's plans, turning the Roman Republic into a Mediterranean empire of 60 million people, and establishing the Pax Romana (Roman Peace) throughout its provinces.*

GLOSSARY

Aedile: *Roman official whose rank was below that of praetor but above quaestor.*

Alexandria: *Graeco-Macedonian port capital of Egypt founded by Ptolemy, one of Alexander the Great's generals. It rivalled Rome's size and magnificence, and was the palatial residence of the ruling Ptolemaic dynasty that ended with Cleopatra's suicide.*

Amphitheatres: *Public buildings which served as arenas for celebrations and displays as well as most famously for contests between gladiators and gladiators and wild animals.*

Asia: *Roman province that covers the area of modern western Turkey.*

Centurion: *Roman army staff officers in charge of between 100 and 1,000 soldiers. Professional military men, and there were normally about 60 centurions in a legion.*

Circus Maximus: *Rome's largest racetrack where 150,000 spectators could watch and bet on chariot races.*

Cisalpine Gaul: *Roman province covering the area that is today northern Itlay.*

Client King: *Rulers of kingdoms beyond the boundaries of the Roman empire who nevertheless owed their positions and allegiance to Rome.*

Cohort: *Roman army unit of which* there were 10 to a legion, each divided into 6 centuries.

Consul: *The supreme elected civil and military office in Rome. Each consulship lasted for one year, though consuls could be re-elected and serve several terms.*

Dictator: *The supreme, and originally temporary Roman office held by an individual in times of emergency. Sulla became Dictator but then resigned, and Caesar held the office three times before becoming Dictator for life. The post was abolished after his death.*

Forum: *The principal public square of a town or city around which were built the main civic buildings and temples.*

Further Spain: *A Roman Province in southern-central Spain whose main cities were Corduba (Cordoba) and Gades (Cadiz). It was flanked by Nearer Spain, and Lusitania (Portugal).*

Gaul: *Roman province of what is today France and Belgium.*

Gladiators: *Usually criminals and prisoners of war, gladiators were highly trained professional killers who fought each other and wild animals for public entertainment in amphitheatres across the Roman empire.*

Illyricum: *Roman province covering area between Bosnia and Albania.*

Imperator: *Title used by Roman*

emperors to indicate their status, and more generally used to salute Roman military commanders after a victory.

Insulae: *The multi-storey apartment blocks where most Romans lived. The term means 'island' because insulae were often surrounded by roads. Crowded and unsanitary, insulae had no running water or sewers.*

Jupiter: *Father of the gods in Roman religion, and in many ways simply the Roman equivalent of the Greek Zeus. He was the protector of Rome and its people.*

Legion: *The main unit of the Roman army. Each legion had 5,000 infantry, 120 cavalry, and auxiliary troops.*

Patrician: *The group of aristocratic Roman families who traced their origins to Rome's earliest days. There were 14 patrician clans composed of 30 families.*

Plebeian: *The mass of non-patrician Roman citizens.*

Praetorian Guard: *The imperial bodyguard created by Augustus and originally composed of 1,000 soldiers.*

Pontifex Maximus: *The most prestigious elected religious office in Rome – literally the highest of all priests. The office was held for life.*

Praetor: *Second in authority only to the Consul. Praetors were state officials. Originally there were 12 praetors of which the most important was the praetor urbanus (city praetor).*

Quaestor: *Lowest office of state that a senator could hold. Quaestors often served as finance officers attached to provincial governor.*

Senate: *The supreme council of the Roman state whose senators were recruited from quaestors. Octavian/Augustus fixed membership at 600, and each senator needed to own property worth 10,000 gold pieces (1 million sesterii).*

Transalpine Gaul: *Roman province covering the area that is today southern France.*

Tribune: *An office which formed part of a plebeian senator's career. Originally, as Tribunes of the People, the office holder was expected to protect Roman citizens by using their vote of veto.*

Triumph: *The grand procession through Rome awarded to a victorious Roman general. The triumph ended at the Temple of Jupiter on the Capitoline Hill. After Octavian/Augustus, triumphs became a monopoly of the emperors.*

Vestal Virgins: *Six Vestal Virgins served the goddess Vesta in her temple next to Rome's Forum. They served for 30 years, during which they were expected to remain virgins.*

INDEX